Days and Times
Los Días y Las Horas

early
temprano

wake up
despertarse

seven o'clock
las siete

morning
la mañana

by Mary Berendes • illustrated by Kathleen Petelinsek

childsworld.com

Published by The Child's World®
800-599-READ • childsworld.com

Copyright © 2024 by The Child's World®
All rights reserved. No part of this book may be reproduced or utilized in any form or by any means without written permission from the publisher.

Language Adviser
Ariel Strichartz

ISBN Information
9781503884823 (Reinforced Library Binding)
9781503885967 (Portable Document Format)
9781503886605 (Online Multi-user eBook)
9781503887244 (Electronic Publication)

LCCN
2023937287

Printed in the United States of America

About the Author

Mary Berendes has authored more than 75 books for children, including nature titles as well as books about parables, fables, countries, and holidays. Mary loves collecting antique books and playing the piano when her twin children allow her some free time. She lives with her family in Minnesota.

About the Illustrator

Kathleen Petelinsek has loved to read and draw since she was a child. As an adult, she has illustrated well over 100 books for children. She also loves animals. Kathleen and her husband live in Wisconsin with their two dogs, one cat, and three chickens.

clock
el reloj
alarm
la alarma
12
1
2
3
4
5
6
7
8
9
10
11
minute hand
el minutero
hour hand
el horario
second hand
el segundero
hour
la hora
second
el segundo
digital clock
el reloj digital
7:00:22 AM
minute
el minuto

morning
la mañana

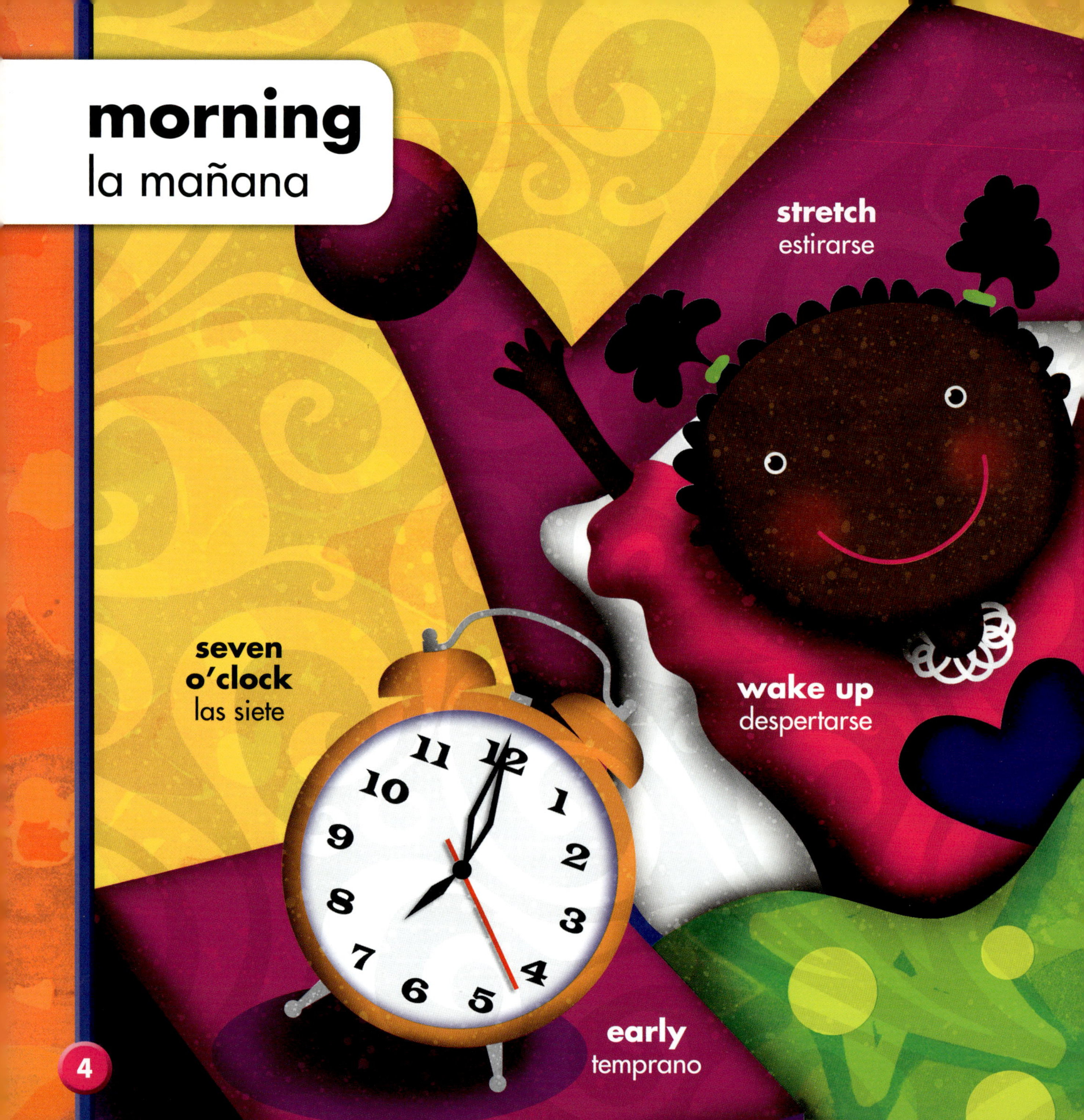

sunrise
la salida del sol

lunchtime
la hora de almorzar
sandwich
el sándwich
milk
la leche

noon
el mediodía

afternoon
la tarde
12
1
2
3
4
5
6
7
8
9
10
11
clock
el reloj
three thirty
las tres y media

sunshine
la luz del sol
playtime
el recreo

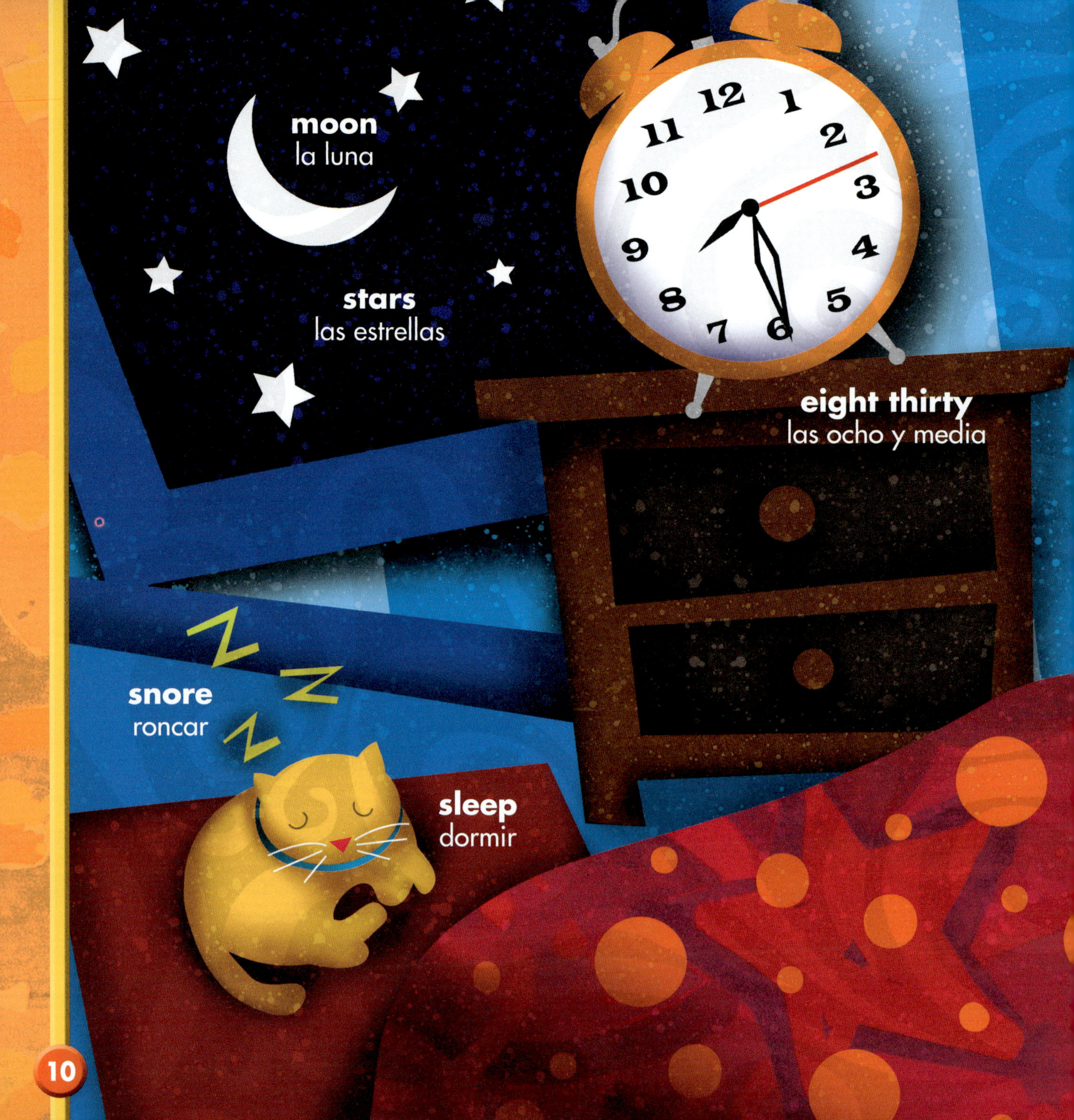
moon
la luna
stars
las estrellas
12
1
2
3
4
5
6
7
8
9
10
11
eight thirty
las ocho y media
snore
roncar
sleep
dormir

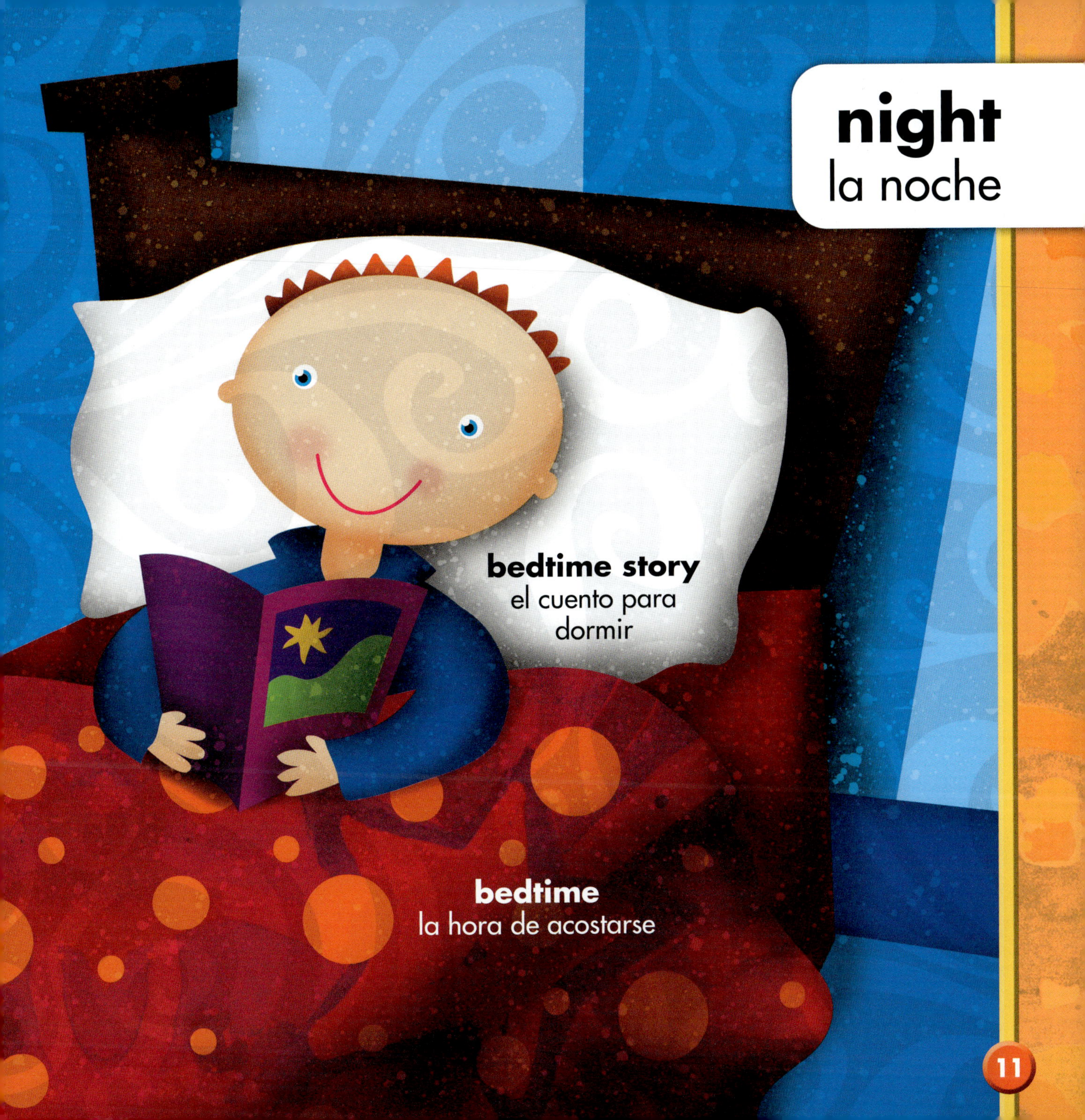
night
la noche
bedtime story
el cuento para
dormir
bedtime
la hora de acostarse

calendar
el calendario

month
el mes

days
los días

5
Saturday
4
11
18
25
dates
las fechas

months
los meses

March
marzo
April
abril
spring
la primavera

spring
la primavera
May
mayo
June
junio
summer
el verano

July
julio
August
agosto

autumn
el otoño

September
septiembre

October
octubre

November
noviembre
December
diciembre
winter
el invierno

workday
la jornada laboral
Monday
lunes
Tuesday
martes

weekdays
los días laborales

school day
el día lectivo

Friday
viernes

Thursday
jueves

Wednesday
miércoles

weekend
el fin de semana

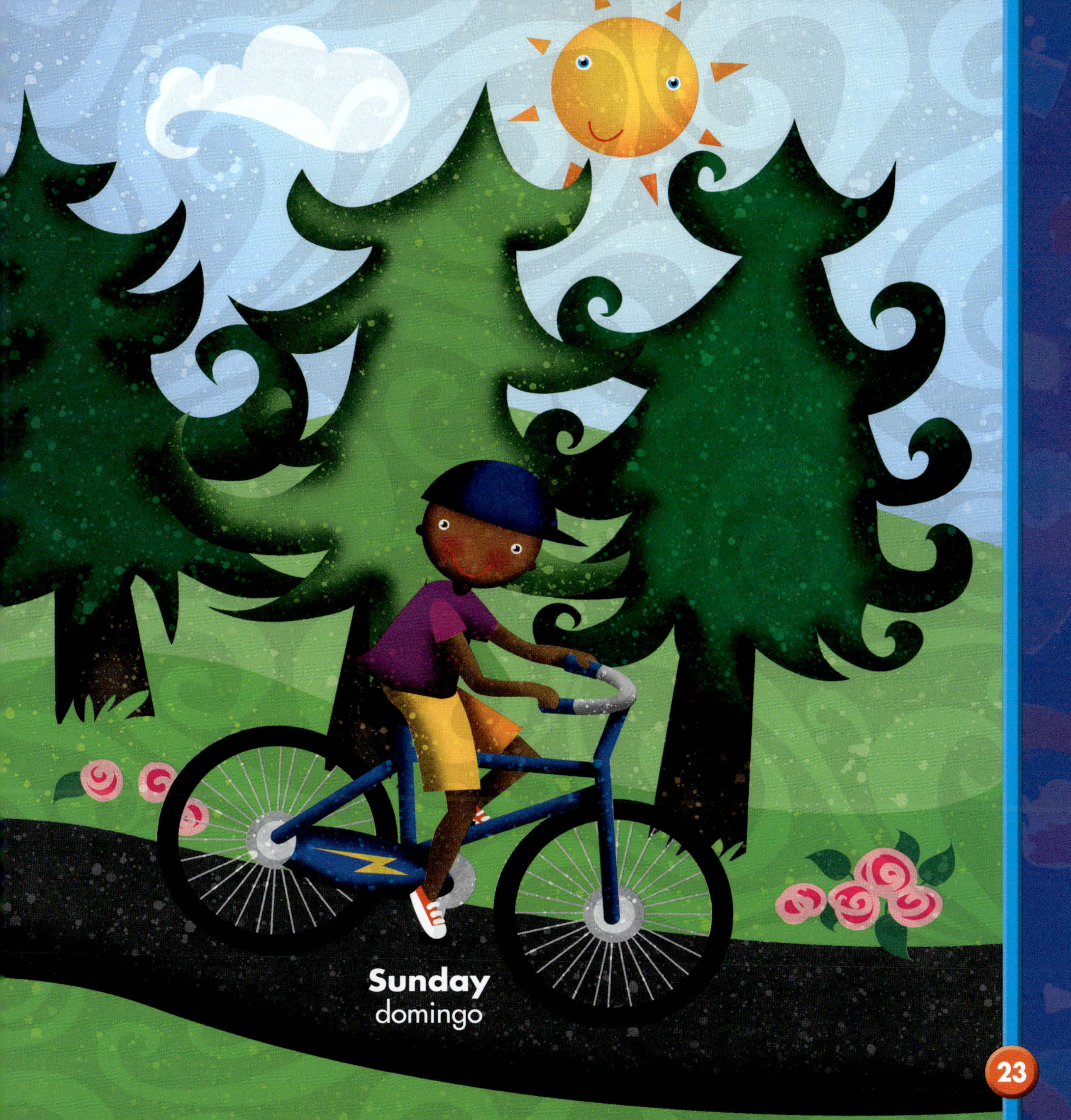

Sunday
domingo

WORD LIST
lista de palabras

afternoon	la tarde
alarm	la alarma
April	abril
August	agosto
autumn	el otoño
bedtime	la hora de acostarse
bedtime story	el cuento para dormir
calendar	el calendario
clock	el reloj
dates	las fechas
days	los días
December	diciembre
digital clock	el reloj digital
early	temprano
eight thirty	las ocho y media
February	febrero
Friday	viernes
hour	la hora
hour hand	el horario
January	enero
July	julio
June	junio
lunchtime	la hora de almorzar
March	marzo
May	mayo
milk	la leche
minute	el minuto
minute hand	el minutero
Monday	lunes
month	el mes
moon	la luna
morning	la mañana
night	la noche
noon	el mediodía
November	noviembre
October	octubre
playtime	el recreo
sandwich	el sándwich
Saturday	sábado
school day	el día lectivo
second	el segundo
second hand	el segundero
September	septiembre
seven o'clock	las siete
to sleep	dormir
to snore	roncar
spring	la primavera
stars	las estrellas
to stretch	estirarse
summer	el verano
Sunday	domingo
sunrise	la salida del sol
sunshine	la luz del sol
three thirty	las tres y media
Thursday	jueves
times	las horas
Tuesday	martes
to wake up	despertarse
Wednesday	miércoles
weekdays	los días laborales
weekend	el fin de semana
winter	el invierno
workday	la jornada laboral
year	el año